DOUBLE Switch

DIANA NOONAN

illustrated by Christine Ross

Chapter 1

It wasn't Jordan Blake's fault that he got mistaken for a spy. He couldn't help it if he was tall and lanky with long legs. And as for his thin, pointy nose ... well, Jordan's dad said it came from Grandpa's side of the family.

"Wasn't Grandpa Casey a spy?" asked Jordan.

"We don't talk about that," said Mr Blake.

"If only I didn't creep everywhere," thought Jordan. He spent hours in front of the mirror working on his walking. But with feet as big as his, it was impossible to walk normally. Every time he looked for a place to put his toes, he'd stop. And as everyone knows, when you stop before every step you take, you don't walk … you creep.

Buying a briefcase was Jordan's own idea. He was always hungry, and a briefcase was a lot better than a backpack for carrying sandwiches and a can of drink. But even with the briefcase, the long nose, and the creepy walk, Jordan Blake might not have looked *quite* so much like a spy if it wasn't for two big problems.

The first problem was his mother. She worried about him from dawn until dusk. She worried about him at night too, but Jordan didn't know that because he was fast asleep. Most of all, his mother worried that he might catch a cold, which was why she made him wear a coat and hat.

"Dress warmly, or you'll catch your death of cold," she told him every morning before he left for school.

"But, Mum," he moaned, "no one wears a coat and hat like this any more."

"This coat and hat belonged to your Grandpa," said his mum. "If it was good enough for him, it's good enough for you."

"But Grandpa Casey was a spy."

"That's enough," said Mrs Blake. "Put on the coat and hat."

Chapter 2

The other big reason why Jordan Blake looked like a spy was Maggie Maddigan. She was enough to give anyone a hunted look. There aren't too many girls who like lanky, thin-nosed boys in large coats and hats, but Maggie was one of them. She followed Jordan everywhere.

"Hey, Jordan!" she called, whenever he least expected it. "Want to help me with my homework? Want to go to the cinema with me? Want to walk the dog with me?"

Jordan hid in the school library. He crept around the bookshelves trying not to be noticed. This made him look even more like a spy.

Jordan didn't care how he looked as long as Maggie didn't find him. But she always did.

After school, on the Friday afternoon that Jordan got mistaken for a spy, Maggie was in the library. She was finding information about zebras for her school project when she saw the collar of Jordan's coat sticking up from behind a shelf.

"Hey, Jordan," she called, "I've been looking for you everywhere! Do you want to come to my birthday party on Saturday?"

Jordan grabbed his briefcase and ran. It was more of a fast creep than a run, but he was out of that library in three seconds flat. In three and a half seconds flat, Maggie was after him.

"We're all going to have pizza," she called. "Don't you want to come?"

Jordan ran like lightning, but Maggie wasn't the sprint champ for nothing. She had almost caught up with him when Jordan got lucky.

Behind him, something twanged. A rubber band from Maggie's braces sprang out of her mouth and went bouncing along the footpath. Maggie had to stop to pick it up. At the same time, Jordan looked up and saw a sign he'd never noticed before. "Café Snoop," he read on the window in front of him. He dived for the door.

Inside, he looked around. "So," he thought, "I'm not the only one to have a coat and hat like Grandpa Casey's after all."

Chapter 3

Jordan put down his briefcase beside the café door. He peered out of the window.

Maggie had gone. Thank goodness! Now he could go home too. He reached for his briefcase, but which one was it? There were five beside the door, and they all looked exactly the same. He gently kicked each case until he heard a clatter. It had to be the drink can! He picked up the briefcase, slipped through the door, and ran down the street as fast as he could.

Just once, on his way home, Jordan was sure he heard footsteps. He hoped it wasn't Maggie again! He ducked into a doorway and looked back. But it was all right. It was just someone he'd seen in Café Snoop. For a minute, Jordan thought the man was waving at him.

At home, Jordan ran upstairs. His tummy was rumbling. He couldn't wait for those sandwiches. He put his briefcase down on the bed. He was just about to open it when he heard a tap, tap at his window. That Maggie! She wouldn't give up!

First she'd tried to chase him home. Now she was trying to get his attention by throwing stones at his window. He'd fix her! He filled a balloon with water from the bathroom tap and waited by the window. The next time he heard the tapping, he opened the window and let the balloon go. **Splat! Scream!** That would teach her.

Jordan looked out of the window. Maggie had gone, but the customer from Café Snoop was standing on the street. He looked as if he'd been in a shower of rain. He waved, and Jordan waved back. He certainly was friendly.

Chapter 4

Jordan went back to the briefcase. He was opening it when the phone rang.

"Jordan!" called Mrs Blake. "Answer that phone, would you?"

"Blakes' house," said Jordan. There was silence.

Jordan tried again. "Can I help you?" he asked.

"Come outside," said a strange, deep voice. "Bring your briefcase. I want to talk to you."

"Oh, yeah?" said Jordan. "No way, Maggie Maddigan. You can't fool me with that voice." He put the phone down. He had better things to do than talk to her. He had his sandwiches waiting for him.

Jordan sat on his bed. He pulled the briefcase onto his lap and pushed down on the locks. The case sprang open. But inside, instead of sandwiches and a drink can, there was a tape recorder. He stared at it for a minute. Then he pressed the "play" button.

"I'll be waiting for you in the park," said a voice. "I'll be by the big oak tree."

He couldn't believe it. That sneaky Maggie! She'd swapped his food for her tape recorder!

Jordan was so angry that he hopped up and down on one foot. He wasn't going to hide any more. He'd go to the park all right. He'd tell Maggie to go away and leave him alone! But what if one of his friends saw him talking to her? He reached for his dark glasses and left the house.

A moment later, Mrs Blake shouted from the house, "Jordan Blake! Put on your coat and hat before you go anywhere!"

Jordan put down his case and went in to get his coat and hat. That was the moment that the man from Café Snoop had been waiting for.

Chapter 5

At the park, Jordan crept past the duck pond. He crept past the children's playground and the rose garden. He was heading for the big trees at the end of the nature trail. In his hand, the briefcase rattled and clicked. Maggie had better have the missing food, or she'd never see her tape recorder again.

It was dim and dark at the end of the nature trail. The branches of the big trees shut out most of the light. Jordan stopped beside a park bench. It was very quiet. There wasn't even a bird chirping.

A dark shape flitted from one tree to another. Jordan put down the briefcase. "Maggie?" he called. "Maggie Maddigan, if that's you, you'd better come out right now." He waited. "I know you're there," he called.

He was just about to take another step forwards when suddenly there was a dreadful racket. Whistles blew, and sirens wailed. "Don't move!" called a voice from the branches above his head. "Stay where you are." Then a whole lot of police officers stepped out from behind the trees. Jordan Blake almost jumped out of his skin.

"Got you at last, Agent X!" said a voice behind Jordan. Snap! Handcuffs closed around his wrists.

"Wait!" he yelled. "You've made a big mistake! I'm not Agent X. I'm Jordan Blake!"

"And I'm the sugarplum fairy," laughed the officer. "I'm afraid that you and your briefcase will have to come along with us."

"Just a minute," said a voice that Jordan knew well. "This isn't Agent X. This is my best friend, Jordan Blake. And I can prove it."

Jordan had never been so pleased to see Maggie Maddigan in all his life.

Chapter 6

From out of her jacket pocket, Maggie took her school photo. "I carry this with me everywhere," she said. "See, there's Jordan."

Jordan's face was circled with a blue ring. Maggie had drawn hearts all around it. "And there's his name," said Maggie. She pointed to the list of class names. "Jordan Blake."

"Good try," said the officer. "But not good enough." She picked up the briefcase. "All the proof we need is in this case."

"In that briefcase you'll find Jordan's sandwiches and a can of drink," said Maggie. "He's always hungry."

Jordan was confused. In that case was Maggie's tape recorder. It was sure to look like spy equipment.

"Let's see, shall we," said the officer. She pressed the locks. The briefcase sprang open, and out fell ... some sandwiches and a can of drink!

"Oh, boy," said the officer. "I think we've made a big mistake."

Chapter 7

Jordan and Maggie got to ride home in the police car. The police officer said she was sorry about a hundred times. She said it to Mrs Blake too.

"Never mind," said Jordan's mum. "Some people thought his Grandpa Casey was a spy too."

"He was, wasn't he?" said Jordan.

"Quiet, Jordan!" said Mrs Blake.

When the officer had gone, Jordan turned to Maggie. "There are a few things I don't understand," he said. "How come there's food in my briefcase instead of your tape recorder?"

"What tape recorder? Why would my tape recorder be in your briefcase?" asked Maggie.

"But wasn't it you who told me to go to the park?" asked Jordan.

"No way," said Maggie.

"Then how did you know I was there?" he asked.

"I followed you, of course," said Maggie. "I follow you everywhere."

Jordan went red.

"Please say you'll come to my birthday party," begged Maggie. "It's going to be a fancy dress party, and you owe me a favour for saving you."

"Well, OK," said Jordan, "but I don't want to dress up."

"You don't have to dress up," said Maggie. "You look like the perfect spy just the way you are!"